COOKING FOR SCOUTS

The 1st Gotham Scout Group Cookbook

Mark Howard

With foreword by Ed Stafford

BillyBooks

Cooking for Scouts | The 1st Gotham Scout Group Cookbook

First published in the United Kingdom in 2018 by BillyBooks, an imprint of BDS21 Ltd, 11 High Street, Ruddington, Notts NG11 6DT

www.billybooks.co.uk

Copyright © BillyBooks 2018

Acknowledgements:
Author / Editor: Mark Howard
Designer: Jason Billin

Images: Front cover image © Charlie Howick; Back cover image © Mark Howard.

Alex Staniforth for p27; **Ben Anderson** for p10, 24; **Charlie Howick** for p17, 25, 31, 38-39, 42-43; **Ed Stafford** for p7 & p45; **Darren Altman / Apollo Photography** for p81; **Dave Watson** for p28; **Dwayne Fields** for p33; **Jenny Howard** for p37, 40-41; **Julie Bailey** for p75, 86; **Kate Whitaker** (recipe image) for p61; **Mark Howard** for p2-3, 4-5, 6, 8, 11, 12-13, 15, 18, 20-21, 30, 34, 48, 54-55, 57, 58, 62-63, 66-67, 71, 72-73, 74, 76-77, 80, 83, 84-85, 87, 88-89, 91, 92-93, 95; **Matt Russell** (Gino D'Acampo) for p61; **Megan Hine** for p19; **Penny Gwynne** for p65; **Picsfive / Shutterstock** for p53; **Sally Bee** for p29; **Scott Heffield / Epic Action Imagery** for p78-79; **Sean Conway** for p46; **Stacey Curzon** for p64; **Val Stones** for p22, 23; **Wayne Sleep** for p40.

BillyBooks will be grateful for any information that will assist them in keeping future editions up-to-date. Although all reasonable care has been taken in the preparation of this book, neither the publishers nor the author / Scout Group can accept any liability for any consequence arising from the use thereof, or the information contained therein.

All recipes in this book have been submitted by the named contributors, who have asserted that they are the copyright holders of the recipes and/or are legally entitled to grant permission for the recipes to be included herein. If you feel that any recipe has been wrongly attributed, please contact the publisher.

All recipes are given as a guide, please use general safety precautions (and common sense) when preparing, cooking and handling food both in and out of the kitchen. Be aware that some recipes contain nuts and many contain wheat gluten.

All recipes included in this publication have been submitted as donations to this book

Views and opinions contained herein are not necessarily those of The Scout Association, but are given by members of our local village Scout Group.

We would like to thank those who have contributed and made this book what it is.

A CIP catalogue record for this book is available from the British Library.

ISBN 978 1 9996555 0 1

Printed in Italy

1 2 3 4 5 6 7 8 9 10

Contents

Foreword

" *Food is an essential part of survival. This book is a compilation of recipes which can be enjoyed both indoors and outdoors, whether that be cooked in the comfort of your home or something to be enjoyed around a warm campfire with friends.*

1st Gotham celebrates 60 years of adventures and making a difference to people in their community.

Just like Scouting, food brings people together and just like Scouting this book is about being together and trying something new.

In the spirit of this book, try a recipe or two, then share it with a friend and with it you'll carry the spirit of Scouting. "

Join the Adventure
Ed Stafford

Introduction

This cookbook has been a really exciting project, I have been in contact with a variety of people requesting a donation of recipes, not all successful but hope you would agree, that we have a great array within this local cookbook. At times, this project has seemed a long journey. However, with a little perseverance and belief, we have finally made it. It would not have been possible if it wasn't for a little help from some amazing people.

Thank you to Jenny, Samuel and Oliver for putting up with my ideas and being super supportive! A massive thank you to Jason Billin of BillyBooks, for the creative side and donation of publishing this book, and to Matt for proofreading everything, you have done a brilliant job! Thank you to Mary and Arthur Howick for preparing and making some of these recipes and then letting us use their home for photographing those recipes.

Thank you to members of 1st Gotham Scout Group, children and young people, leaders, parents/carers, past and present Executive Committee members and those who have been involved with the group in some capacity. Also, thank you to our leaders who give timeless hours of voluntary work week-in and week-out and make such a difference to our community. Thank you to Ed Stafford for the foreword and recipe.

Thank you to everyone else who has contributed by donating a recipe to this collection (alphabetical first name order):

Alex Staniforth; Alison Hammond; Alison Harrison; Andrew Bassford; Andrew Symth; Ben Anderson; Charlie Howick; Cherry and Chris O'Grady; Chris Howard; Brodie and Dan Johnson; Darren Altman; Dave Watson; Dwayne Fields; Elizabeth; Gino D'Acampo; Helen Lomas; Jayne Torvill; Jenny Howard; Jo Brand; Judy and Pete Nelson; Julie Bailey; Kate Bottley; Kathryn Wills; Kevin Nolan; Lorena; Lorraine Kelly; Mark Dennison; Mary Howick; Matthew; Megan Hine; Natalie LaTouche; Pam Towers; Penny Gwynne; Phil Howick; Rick Stein; Robert Lindsley; Salasi Gbormittah; Sally Bee; Samuel Howard; Scott Haffield; Sean Conway; Sharron Davies; Stacey Curzon; Steffan LaTouche; Sue Lyme-Brewin; The Garlic Farm on the Isle of Wight (Natasha Edwards); Tim Kidd; Val Stone and Wayne Sleep.

Also thank you to those from the Retro Recipe Book (1979): Anne; Mary; Molly; Olive; Sheila; Sybil and Teresa.

Thank you to those who have supported this project during the various stages.

Finally again, thank you Jason for making this 1st Gotham Scout Group Cookbook a reality.

Mark

Pitching Camp
Starters

It's the staple garlic side order. We take our garlic bread pretty seriously. We've tried and tested so many variations and only the best make the grade. This one takes garlic bread to a whole new level. You don't have to add the cheese if you prefer the purist version.

The paprika adds the perfect final touch for flavour and colour. You won't get a better one.

The Best Cheesy Garlic Bread

The Garlic Farm on The Isle of Wight

Ingredients

- *1 baguette*
- *100g butter*
- *3-4 large garlic cloves, crushed*
- *100g mozzarella ball*
- *100g any hard, strong cheese (cheddar works well)*
- *Handful of any combination of fresh parsley, rosemary, basil or marjoram*
- *Paprika for sprinkling*

Method

- Preheat the oven to 200°C. Add all the filling ingredients to a food processor until completely mixed.
- Cut diagonal slices into the baguette about 2/3 way through so the loaf is still intact.
- Use a flat knife to spread the filling generously in between the slices.
- Loosely wrap the bread in foil sealing the ends and top. Cut baguette into two pieces to fit in the oven if necessary.
- Bake for 20-25 mins until all the filling is melted. For the last 5 mins, open the foil, sprinkle over the paprika and brown the top.

  Serve immediately.

from *The Garlic Farm Cookbook*
published by The Garlic Press

Tomato and Basil Soup

Mary Howick - Gotham Stalwart & Supercook

Ingredients

1kg large red tomatoes,
   preferably off the vine
Large onions, peeled and sliced
A handful of basil leaves
A little oil
1 litre of vegetable stock,
   using 2 x Knorr® vegetable stock
   cubes
25g butter
1 tbsp cornflour
Salt and pepper to taste

Method

- Put the tomatoes in a large bowl and cover with boiling water. Stand for 5 mins then remove the skins. Cut in half and squeeze out the seeds.
- In a large pan, add the oil and onions. Cook gently until softened (don't brown them).
- Add the tomatoes, basil leaves and stock. Cook until the tomatoes have softened.
- Blitz well with a blender.
- Melt butter and mix in cornflour. Whisk this into the tomatoes and heat again until thickened slightly.
- Season to taste.

Dippy Orange Egg

Mark Howard - Group Scout Leader, Assistant Beaver Scout Leader & Explorer Scout Leader (all-round good egg)

Ingredients

- Egg (1 per orange)
- Oranges
- Bread

Method

- Using a campfire, get a good bed of embers
- Take the top off the orange and core out the flesh (middle) to about an egg size. You can save this to make a fresh orange drink to accompany your dippy egg.
- Crack open the egg and pour into your cored orange.
- Place upright on the embers and cook until you are happy with the egg - usually about 5 minutes.
- Take your bread and cut into "soldiers" - white fluffy bread may be best!
- Carefully remove the orange - don't burn yourself!
- Dip your soldiers into your Dippy Orange Egg and enjoy!

A different variation to Dippy Eggs and Soldiers, in this recipe you use an orange to cook your egg!

13

Welsh Rarebit

Robert Lindsay - Actor

Ingredients

Mature cheddar cheese
Salt and Pepper
Guinness®
Worcestershire Sauce®
Bread

Method

- Welsh Rarebit is best made by grating some mature cheddar cheese and adding some salt and pepper.
- Mix to a paste with some Guinness® and and add a bit of Worcester Sauce®.
- Then toast one side of the bread and cover the other side with the mixture and grill until golden brown and bubbling.
  Delicious!

Steamed Mussels with Tomato and Tarragon

Rick Stein CBE - Chef

Ingredients

- *1 kg mussels*
- *30 ml dry white wine*
- *60 g tomatoes, peeled, deseeded and finely chopped*
- *5 g French tarragon, finely chopped*
- *30 ml extra virgin olive oil*
- *2 cloves garlic, finely chopped*
- *30 g unsalted butter*

Method

- Make sure the mussels are tightly closed. If they are fresh-farmed ones there is no need to wash them, but if they are showing any signs of grit or sand wash them in copious amounts of cold water.
- Take a large saucepan, add the olive oil and garlic and soften over a medium heat for about a minute. Add the mussels, turn up the heat and add the white wine.
- Put a lid on the pan and cook for a few minutes until all the shells have opened, but only just. Stir the shells once or twice during the cooking to distribute them evenly. Remove and pour through a colander set over a bowl.
- Keep the mussels warm while you transfer the liquor to a pan, heat until boiling, whisk in the butter then add the tomato and tarragon. Check the seasoning; it's always a good idea to leave seasoning to the end with shellfish because you never know how salty they are going to be, then add salt if necessary and freshly ground black pepper.
- Add the mussels back into the pan. Serve with plenty of crusty bread or alternatively with a mound of al dente linguine pasta.

Dutch Oven Parmesan Bread

Mark Howard

Ingredients

- *2 cups of strong white flour*
- *3/4 cups of water*
- *1/2 tsp yeast*
- *1tsp sugar*
- *1tsp salt*
- *Vegetable oil*
- *35 g parmesan cheese*
- *Based on Dutch Oven size 1.8L*

Method

- Mix the flour, yeast, sugar, 30 g of Parmesan and salt with warm water. Once mixed, this should be springy to touch. Cover and leave to prove for 1 hour.
- After 1 hour, re-shape into a ball using floured board.
- Then place in oiled Dutch Oven, allow to prove for a further 30 minutes.
- Sprinkle 5 g of Parmesan over the top of the dough and score.
- Pre-heat oven at 195°C (fan assisted).
- Place in oven and cook with lid on for 25 minutes.
- Remove the Dutch Oven lid and cook for further 10 minutes.
- The temperature inside the bread should be around 90°C.
- The bread should be golden in colour. Allow to cool and enjoy!

Alternative

- This can also be cooked on an open fire either by hanging the pot on a tripod and allowing a good 1hr or so to cook, or the Dutch Oven can be placed on hot embers, and, again, allow a good 1hr to cook. Embers can be carefully placed on the lid, this can speed up the cooking time slightly. But cooking times will vary.

Leek Cannelloni with Thyme and Cheese Sauce

Mary Howick

Ingredients

Cheese Sauce (cheating)

- *25 g butter*
- *250 ml full fat milk*
- *1 packet Colmans white sauce mix*
- *2 tbsp double cream*
- *75 g Gruyere cheese, grated*

Tomato sauce

- *1 tbsp oil*
- *1 small onion, finely chopped*
- *1 garlic clove, crushed*
- *200 g chopped tomatoes*
- *5 ml red wine vinegar*
- *2 tsp caster sugar*

Cannelloni

- *50 g butter*
- *450 g leeks, chopped*
- *2 cloves garlic, crushed*
- *2 tsp thyme*
- *2 tbsp water*
- *250 g ricotta*
- *250 g lasagne sheets*

Method

- Heat oven to 200°C.

Cheese Sauce

- Melt butter, stir in white sauce mix, add milk and mix. Heat to thicken, beat in cream and gruyere.

Tomato Sauce

- Heat oil, add onion and garlic and cook until softened. Add tomatoes and simmer for 15-20 mins until thickened. Put the vinegar in a small pan and reduce to 1 tsp. Stir into tomato sauce and spoon over a dish.

Cannelloni

- Melt butter, add leeks, garlic, thyme and water. Cook gently uncovered for 15 mins until leeks are tender. Cool and beat in ricotta then season.

Pasta

- Cook pasta sheets in boiling water until soft. Drain and cool.

To assemble

- Spoon leek filling along one edge of lasagne sheets and roll up. Arrange on top of tomato sauce in dish. Pour over the cheese sauce and bake for 20 mins until golden.

Lovely!

Leek Cannelloni with Thyme and Cheese Sauce

Pork and Prawn Wontons

Steffan LaTouche

Ingredients

- *250g pork mince*
- *150g raw king prawns*
- *100g dried shiitake mushrooms*
- *3 tbsp light soy sauce*
- *1 tbsp rice wine / Shaoxing rice wine*
- *1 tbsp sesame oil*
- *1 tsp cornflour*
- *1 large pinch of salt*
- *1 large pinch of ground white pepper*
- *1 tsp sugar*
- *1 pack wonton skins / wrappers*
- *groundnut oil for frying*
  (use alternative if allergic to nuts)

Method

- Rehydrate the mushrooms for 20 minutes, then chop into small dice.
- Chop raw prawns.
- In a large bowl, mix ALL ingredients together and leave to marinate for at least 30 minutes, overnight is best.
- Open wonton skin packet, take 1 skin and place a teaspoon of filling mixture in the middle. With your finger wet the edge of the wonton skin, then pull all four sides together to create a parcel shape, repeat until all the mix has gone!
- Heat oil, fry until golden (test first for oil temperature and cooking time), serve with sweet chilli sauce.

I have chosen this recipe that my Chinese mum taught me. It's a family favourite. During Chinese New Year, Won Tons are eaten because they resemble bags of gold – which to the Chinese is good luck.

Cheesy Campfire Twists

Mark Howard

Ingredients

- *1 cup of self-raising flour*
- *2 tsp caster sugar*
- *1 tsp butter*
- *100ml water*
- *Pinch of salt*
- *Grated mature cheese (zester sized holed cheese grater)*
- *Skewers or green tree twigs (peel the bark away) with one end trimmed to a point. (Ash, Willow etc.)*

Makes 3 reasonable sized Twists.

Method

- Place skewers into cool water, to discourage from burning (optional).
- Put the flour in a bowl and combine with the caster sugar, butter, pinch of salt, grated cheese and water.
- Mix using a fork then knead using your hands until it has a dough-like texture, then make into a ball (you may be required to add a drop more water).
- Once it's all combined and the butter is evenly mixed in, split into three smaller balls and roll out into sausage shapes.
- Twist the dough around the skewer (twig).
- Hold over campfire embers, slowly rotating until golden brown.
- Once golden, remove from the heat, allow to cool slightly and enjoy.

Alternative

- Remove the cheese and eat as a plain Twist accompanied with chocolate spread, strawberry jam or peanut butter.
- Try adding your chocolate spread, strawberry jam or peanut butter into the dough before Twisting it around the skewer.

 This is a classic Campfire Treat, which is extra yummy with the cheese!

Wild Garlic & Pine-nut Pesto

Megan Hine - Survival Expert - Scout Ambassador

Ingredients

- *2 handfuls of fresh wild garlic leaves*
- *200 ml extra virgin olive oil*
- *50 g pine nuts*

Method

- Wash or blanch the leaves in boiling water for about 10 seconds and immediately refresh in cold water.
- Place wild Garlic leaves, oil and pine nuts into a food processor until a puree is created.
- Season with salt and peeper to taste
- At this stage you can either transfer straight into a glass jar or add 50 g grated parmesan cheese and then place into a jar. I personally prefer it without the cheese but I know others love the combination of flavours.
- The pesto will freeze well for enjoyment after the Ramsons season is over.

This has to be hands-down one of my favourite wild food recipes.

Why it is I couldn't tell you, but if you like garlic you will love this! I originally created this recipe when I was instructing for a Bushcraft company in Dorset and working with an amazing medicinal herbalist. It goes well with so many dishes or just spread on toast.

The wild garlic in the British countryside is fat, lush and ready to forage in Early to mid spring. Also known as Ramsons, Allium ursinum (bear's garlic) is widespread across Europe liking deciduous, moist, slightly acidic areas. The whole plant can be eaten and the early shoots make a great pickle.

When collecting make sure you ID the plant correctly. I have found poisonous plants such as Dog's Mercury (which looks very similar) grow in amongst the garlic.

If you are collecting the roots make sure you take the whole plant so as to have a way to ID which plant the roots have come from.

Baked Camembert with Garlic and Rosemary

Mark Howard

Ingredients

- *1 x 500g Camembert*
- *Garlic clove*
- *Sprigs of rosemary*
- *Butter*
- *Crusty bread / baguette*
- *Red onion chutney (homemade or bought)*

Method

- Remove all the plastic and packaging from the Camembert and place the Camembert back in the wooden container.
- Start by cutting the garlic cloves into little chunks.
- Then, using a sharp knife, cut slits into the top of the Camembert and place the cut garlic into the slit.
- Wash the sprigs of rosemary, cut off the leaves and, again, place the leaves into the slits next to the garlic.
- Once the garlic and rosemary has been placed in all the slits, place the Camembert sand wooden container on a oven-proof tray and cook at 180°C for 20 minutes.
- While the Camembert is cooking, crush up more garlic cloves and finely chop the Rosemary. Then, mix this in with a good knob of butter (You can either heat the butter to melt it together or just spread this on the toasted bread).
- Slice up some crusty bread/baguette, add the butter mix once toasted.
- By this time the Camembert should be gooey.
- Serve with the toasted bread.
- Spoon gooey Camembert onto the toasted bread slices, add some red onion chutney and enjoy!

A simple but tasty combination!

Cheese, Herb and Sun Blush Tomato Tear & Share Bread

Val Stones - GBBO 2016 – www.bakerval.com

Ingredients

- *800g strong white bread flour*
- *25g light soft brown sugar*
- *175ml warm water (body heat)*
- *175ml whole milk (body heat)*
- *21g instant yeast*
- *60ml olive oil plus a little extra for work surface and oiling proving bowl*
- *30-50g sun blush tomatoes, more or less depending on how much you like them*
- *250g cheddar cheese (retain 50g for sprinkling on the bread before baking)*
- *2 tbsp finely chopped thyme*
- *2 tbsp finely chopped parsley*
- *2 tbsp finely chopped basil, chives can be used instead*
- *75g unsalted, melted butter for brushing on dough before rolling*

Method

- In a bowl combine the flour, salt, and sugar.
- In a large bowl or jug place the warm water, milk and whisk in the yeast until dissolved, leave for two minutes.
- Make a well in the flour mixture, add the liquid to the dry ingredients and then add the olive oil. Mix well with a wooden spoon for two minutes and add a little warm water to make a soft, but not sticky, dough if needed. Leave to rest for five minutes.
- Transfer the dough to a work surface and knead for five minutes until the dough forms a smooth, soft but not sticky ball. Place a little oil in a clean bowl and roll the dough around the bowl until it is coated.
- Cover with a clean tea towel and leave in a warm place to prove for an hour or until almost double in size.
- Whilst the dough is proving, grate the cheese. Finely chop the sun blush tomatoes. Finely chop the herbs of your choice. Grease a 20cm springform baking pan with melted butter.
- Turn the dough out onto a lightly floured work surface and knock back gently (this means to knock out any large air pockets, you can hear the dough "squeak" as you do this).
- Form the dough into a rough rectangle and roll out into a rectangle shape around 30cm x 40cm.
- Brush the dough lightly with melted butter, scatter the herbs over the dough followed by the tomatoes and lastly the cheese.
- Lightly press down the filling mixture with your hand and then begin to roll up the dough evenly towards you, dampen the edge of the dough nearest to you with a little more butter and then nip the edge of the dough to seal.
- With your hands, smooth the roll to make sure it is even.
- Cut the ends off of the roll and set aside, mark the roll into 3cm pieces and either using a sharp knife or dental floss cut the pieces and place the rolls in the baking pan cut side up, place the end pieces in a smaller tin and bake for "testers".

- Leave in a warm place covered with a clean tea towel for about an hour or until almost double in size.
- Preheat the oven to 200°C (190°C for fan assisted) or gas mark 6.
- When the dough is almost doubled in size brush with melted butter and sprinkle with the remaining cheese.
- Place in the oven and bake for 25 minutes and check. If it's browning too quickly, cover with foil and bake for a further 10 minutes.
- The bread is baked when the internal temperature is 185°F using a baking probe. If you haven't got one the bread should be fully baked after 35 minutes, remove from the oven and leave to rest for 2 minutes.
- Run a sharp knife to loosen around the edges, turn out onto a cooling rack and leave to cool for an hour or at least half an hour (if you can't wait).
- Serve with a picnic or just enjoy.
- This bread can be kept fresh for two days or it can be foil wrapped and frozen for up to one month.

Food
Shaped
Mains

Risotto Verde

Sue Lymn-Brewin - Head Teacher, Gotham Primary School

Ingredients

- 6 fl oz (175 ml) Arborio rice (measured in a measuring jug)
- 2 1/2 oz (60 g) butter
- 1 small onion, chopped finely
- 3 fl oz (75 ml) dry white wine
- 18 fl oz (500 ml) vegetable stock
- Small bunch of fresh sage, chopped
- 4 oz (110 g) baby broad beans, cooked and then popped from their skins
- Pack of asparagus, cut into pieces
- 1 bunch spring onions, chopped
- 2 tbsp parmesan cheese, freshly grated
- 1 bunch fresh chives chopped
- Salt and freshly ground black pepper to taste

Method

- Melt the butter in a large saucepan, sweat the chopped onion in the pan for 5-7 minutes over a moderate heat.
- Add the rice to the pan, and stir to combine with the butter.
- Add the white wine, vegetable stock, chopped sage, 1/2 a teaspoon of salt and some freshly ground black pepper.
- Heat until simmering, then stir once and put the lid on.
- Turn the heat to low and cook for 15 minutes.
- After the 15 minutes are up, remove from the heat and stir in the broad beans, the chopped asparagus and the chopped spring onions.
- Add the grated parmesan cheese, and gently stir everything together.
- Return the pan to the heat, put the lid back on and cook the risotto for another 5 minutes.
- Stir in the chives and serve immediately with additional freshly grated parmesan cheese.

We were in a lovely restaurant in the market square in Bruges, Brussels when we first ate a version of this dish.

We sat outside watching the bustle of the busy market square and the day and this dish were just perfect!

I adapted this recipe from several I have found.

This is a fabulous starter and every time I have served it everyone loves it as much as I do! Enjoy!

Sweet Chilli Chicken Stir Fry

Alex Staniforth - Adventurer

Ingredients (serves 4)

- *12 boneless chicken thighs (3 each)*

For the stir fry

- *400g medium or long grain brown rice*
- *200g mangetout*
- *200g baby corn*
- *1 tbsp olive oil*

For the sauce

- *100ml light soy sauce*
- *3 tbsp sweet chilli sauce*
- *1/2 inch shredded fresh ginger root*
- *3 garlic cloves, crushed*
- *1 large red chilli, chopped without seeds*
- *Large pinch salt and pepper*

Method

- Preheat the oven to 200° C.
- Add the rice to a large sauce pan and add about 2 1/4 times as much water.
- Bring to the boil then reduce the heat, cover and simmer gently for 35-40 minutes until tender and most of the water is absorbed. Check regularly to ensure the rice doesn't dry out or stick to the pan – add more water if needed. Drain and leave to cool.
- Meanwhile, arrange the chicken thighs in a single layer in a large non-stick roasting tin.
- For the sauce, mix the ingredients together in a small bowl and pour over the chicken. If you have time, leave the chicken to marinate for up to an hour.
- Bake in the oven for 30-35 minutess or until cooked through. Pour half of the sweet chilli sauce into a jug.

For the stir-fry

- Heat 1 tbsp olive oil in a large wok and fry the vegetables on a medium heat for 5 minutes.
- Reduce the heat then stir in the cooked rice and the jug of sweet chilli sauce. Cook for 2 minutes then remove from the heat.
- Portion the stir-fry onto four plates with the cooked chicken thighs and spoon over the remaining sauce to serve.

Tips

- Use whichever vegetables you like in the stir-fry - mushrooms, onions, peppers and pak choi would work well too. It's a great way to use up any leftovers.
- You could also use noodles or white rice, or even microwaveable rice to save time!
- The chillies only give a mild heat but you could remove (or increase!) this if you like.

Cooking for me needs to be simple, cheap and convenient. For an athlete or anyone with an active lifestyle this recipe is not only healthy but filling and very high in protein. It's very flexible so you can easily swap ingredients and quantities to make use of what you already have – minimal waste, maximum taste!

Trout Wrapped in Burdock Leaves

Dave Watson - Woodland Survival Crafts

Ingredients

- *1 medium sized trout, gutted but with head and tail on*
- *Large burdock leaves*
- *Wild garlic or wild cress leaves*

Method

- Get a good fire going so that you have a head of embers that will last the duration of cooking (which is 16-20 minutes).
- Stuff some chopped Ramson (wild garlic) or cress leaves inside the fish.
- Place the trout onto the first burdock leaf and wrap it up as best you can.
- With the other leaf go from the other side and cover the trout, tucking the ends of the leaves in as best as you can.
- Place the parcel onto the embers so that the flaps of the leaves are facing down.
- With a medium sized fish you will want 8 minutes either side but with a larger trout it can be up to 10 minutes either side.
- Use a thick glove to turn the fish over quickly and confidently.
- It is important that the embers are good enough for the second side so planning is important.
- Take the parcel out and remove the top leaf.
- You should find that the skin partly comes away with the leaf.
- With a fork you can section out little fillets whilst avoiding the bones.
- Peel away the tail to reveal the lower section.

Sweet and Sour Pineapple Chicken

This dish is much healthier than a take-away and actually is ready much quicker than it takes a delivery to arrive!

Sally Bee - Chef

Ingredients

- *150g basmati rice*
- *1 tbsp sesame oil*
- *2 skinless chicken breast fillets cut into strips*
- *1 tbsp tomato paste*
- *1 tbsp white wine vinegar*
- *4 spring onions chopped*
- *1 tbsp honey*
- *1 red pepper, cut into strips*
- *125g fresh pineapple cut into chunks*
- *2 cm grated fresh ginger*
- *1/2 tsp Chinese 5 spice power*
- *2 tbsp light soy sauce*
- *6 cherry tomatoes*

Serves 2

Method

- Start by cooking the rice according to the packet instructions – drain and set aside.
- Using a large non-stick frying pan, heat the sesame oil, add the chicken strips and stir fry for 5 minutes. Remove from the pan and set aside.
- Next add the spring onions, the red pepper, pineapple and cherry tomatoes into the pan and fry for 2-3 minutes.
- Reduce the heat and add the ginger, soy sauce, tomato paste, 5 spice powder, white wine vinegar and honey to the pan and simmer for 2-3 minutes.
- Now return the chicken to the pan and heat through until thoroughly hot.
- Serve on top of the rice in 2 bowls.

Perfect Pizza!

Lorena - 1st Gotham Cub Scout

Ingredients

Base

- 5 fl oz warm water
- 1/2 tsp sugar
- 2 tsp dried yeast
- 8 oz strong flour (white or wholemeal)
- 1 tsp salt

Sauce

- 3 tbsp tomato puree
- 1 tsp dried mixed herbs
- 3 tbsp water

Toppings - any of:

- Mushrooms
- onion
- ham
- peppers
- olives
- fresh basil
- fresh tomatoes
- sausage
- pepperoni
- cheese
- mozzarella

Method

- Mix sugar and yeast into water and let it sit until foamy (approx. 5 mins).
- Mix flour and salt into a large bowl.
- Add yeast mixture to dry ingredients.
- Turn dough onto floured surface and knead for 5 mins then let it rest for 5 mins.
- Divide into two and roll out.
- Mix sauce ingredients together and spread onto pizza bases.
- Bake at 230°C for 5 mins.
- Add toppings and cheese and bake for a further 7-10 mins.

This is my favourite thin and crispy pizza!

This salad is made in minutes and is so easy to whip up.

You can buy ready cooked brown rice in tins or cook a batch yourself.

Don't nibble on any extra cashews!

Tropical Cashew Nut Rice Salad With Mango

Lorraine Kelly - TV Personality

Ingredients

- *4 heaped tablespoons of cooked brown rice*
- *1 tbsp (15 g) of salted cashew nuts*
- *1 fresh mango (peeled)*
- *Juice of a lemon*
- *1 tbsp of chopped parsley*
- *1 tbsp of chopped chives*
- *1/2 red pepper*
- *Small bunch of spring onions finely sliced*
- *Lettuce leaves to serve with the salad*
- *Salt and pepper*

  350 calories - 10 g fat

Method

- Heat a small frying pan on a moderate heat and roughly chop the cashew nuts on a board.
- Place the nuts in the heated frying pan to heat up slightly. This releases more flavour from the nuts, so cuts down on the amount you have to use.
- Meanwhile, cut the mango flesh into small cubes, along with the red pepper.
- Mix the two ingredients in a bowl with the cooked brown rice.
- Now add the chopped chives, spring onions, parsley, lemon juice and continue to mix.
- Once the cashew nuts have toasted slightly, mix half of them into the salad and reserve the remainder for garnishing the top.
- Season to taste and serve in a suitable serving bowl with some lettuce garnish and, finally sprinkle with the reserved cashew nuts.

Kevin's Kickin' Chicken

Kevin Nolan - Notts County Manager

Ingredients

- 6 x 4oz skinless boneless chicken breasts
- 1 tablespoon olive oil
- 1/2 teaspoon black pepper
- 1 tablespoon tomato paste
- 1 clove of garlic (crushed)
- 1 cup chicken broth
- 1/4 cup balsamic vinegar
- 1 tablespoon spring onions (chopped)
- 1 tablespoon honey

Method

- Heat oil in a large frying pan.
- Add chicken; brown on all sides (approx 10 minutes).
- Remove from pan, drain off excess fat.
- Add remaining ingredients to pan and bring to a boil.
- Return chicken to the pan and reduce heat.
- Simmer for 30 minutes. Serve.

I don't consider myself to be a very competent chef, and I also don't like it when you have to buy in a load of strange herbs and spices that you find you never use again, but this is an easy recipe with basic ingredients that even I can manage!

It's really tasty and relatively healthy too, so it's something that I can rustle together quite quickly during the pre-season weeks when I am working hard to be fit for the season ahead.

Lamb Burgers

Mary Howick

Ingredients

- 400g lamb mince
- 2 tsp chopped rosemary
- 1 red onion, finely chopped
- 1 garlic clove, crushed
- 1 tbsp oil
- 4 tbsp redcurrant jelly
- 4 wholemeal burger rolls
- 2 sliced tomatoes
- Cucumber slices
- Lettuce
- Burger relish

Method

- Combine lamb mince, onion, garlic and redcurrant jelly and shape into burgers.
- Heat oil in pan and cook burgers slowly until cooked through turning halfway.
- Halve rolls and lightly toast.
- Put burgers in rolls with tomato, cucumber, lettuce and relish.

Jamaican Fried Dumplings

Dwayne Fields - Arctic Adventurer - Scout Ambassador

Ingredients

- *350g Self raising flour*
- *1 tsp Salt*
- *1-2 tbsp Butter*
- *Cup of cold water*
- *Cooking oil*

Should make 7-8 fried dumplings.

Method

- Pour 350g of flour into a medium/large mixing bowl.
- Add a tea spoon of salt to the flour and mix well.
- Add one-two table spoons of butter and continue mixing.
- When the butter is completely mixed in with the flour continue mixing.
- Slowly add water to the mixture until a dough is formed.
- When the ingredients come together in a well-mixed dough, leave it to sit for 15-20 minutes in a cool place.
- Pour your preferred cooking oil (I prefer to use coconut oil) in a flat frying pan. The oil should have a depth of about 3-5millimeters.
- Place the frying pan on a low-medium heat and allow the oil to heat up.
- While the pan/oil is heating up, prepare your dumplings.
- Take handfuls of dough and role them into the rough shape and size of a gulf ball, when this is done, press it into the general shape of a hockey puck.
- Carefully place each dumpling into the frying pan.
- After 4-5 minutes check to see that the underside of the dumplings are golden brown, if they are, turn them over and allow them to fry for a further 3-4 minutes, (they tend to brown faster on the second side as they are already hot).
- Remove them from the pan and place on a paper napkin to remove excess oil.

I'm Dwayne Fields, an Arctic adventurer, outdoor enthusiast and a proud Scout ambassador. This recipe is something I remember and cherish from my early childhood in Jamaica, it's quick, its simple and for us (my family), most importantly it was cheap.

Jamaicans tend to serve fried dumplings as part of a breakfast menu but it can accompany any meal, in reality they're often found on the dinner plate as well. The fact that they can be eaten hot or cold means that there's no prep work needed once they're cooked and are a great treat as a midday snack which isn't full of sugar and other preservatives.

There are many ways to cook fried dumplings; this is my favorite.

My Chilli con Carne

Mary Howick

Ingredients

- *1 tbsp olive oil*
- *1 kg ground minced beef*
- *500g chopped onions*
- *250g bacon lardons*
- *3 garlic cloves, crushed*
- *1 stick celery, diced*
- *3 chillies, seeded and chopped finely*
- *1 bay leaf*
- *1 tbsp ground oregano and cumin*
- *1/2 tbsp ground coriander*
- *1/2 tbsp cayenne pepper*
- *1/2 tsp ground cinnamon*
- *1 can (400g) chopped tomatoes*
- *1 pint beef stock*
- *1 tbsp tomato puree*
- *1 can red kidney beans*
- *Pepper to season*

Method

- Heat oil in large pan and brown mince lightly. Remove and set aside. Add bacon to pan with garlic, celery, chilli, herbs, cumin and corriander. Cook until softened.

- Return meat to pan and add cayenne, cinnamon, chopped tomatoes, stock and tomato puree. Simmer gently for about 1 ½ hours. Keep covered with juices.

- Drain and rinse kidney beans and add to the pan. Cook for another ½ hour.

- Just before serving, fold in some coriander leaves and serve with chopped onions.

My Lamb Curry

Mary Howick

Ingredients

- *2 tbsp oil*
- *1 kg cubed lamb*
- *2 large onions, chopped*
- *4 garlic cloves, crushed*
- *1 tbsp grated ginger*
- *1 tbsp turmeric*
- *1 1/2 tbsp ground cumin*
- *1 tbsp chilli powder or 3 chillies, deseeded and chopped*
- *2 tbsp plain flour*
- *1 box chopped tomatoes*
- *400 g can coconut milk*
- *1 pint of lamb or beef stock*
- *200 g plain yoghurt*

Method

- Heat oil in pan, add lamb and gently brown. Remove with a slotted spoon.
- Add a little more oil to the pan and put in onions, garlic and ginger. Cook slowly until softened (don't brown).
- Add all the spices and flour and mix well. Return lamb to the pan, add coconut milk and tomatoes.
- Cover and simmer gently until lamb is tender. Alternatively, this can be done in a crock pot (slow cooker).
- To serve, add the plain yoghurt and gently heat.

Lemon & Garlic Chicken

Mark Dennison - Radio Presenter

Ingredients

- *Chicken thighs*
- *Garlic cloves (half chopped, the other half whole)*
- *White wine*
- *Thyme*
- *2 lemons*
- *Chicken stock*
- *Pilau rice*
- *More chicken stock*
- *Chopped onion*

Method

- Brown the chicken thighs in a frying pan (skin side down).
- Place in a dish and put in the oven at 180°C.
- In the frying pan, add a dash of white wine, then zest & juice of 2 lemons.
- Throw in the stock, thyme and garlic and pour this liquid over chicken – continue to bake in the oven for around 40 minutes.
- Using the same frying pan, fry the chopped onion, add the rice and stir for around 3 minutes.
- Transfer into a dish, add stock and bake in the oven for around 25-30 minutes.

Beef and Bean Casserole with Redcurrant Jelly
for a slow cooker

Pam Towers - 1st Gotham Scout Group Exec Member

Ingredients

- *1 tbsp oil*
- *1 tbsp plain flour, sieved*
- *800g casserole beef, in chunks*
- *1 tsp mixed herbs*
- *2 medium carrots, thinly sliced*
- *1 medium parsnip, thinly sliced*
- *1 large onion, thinly sliced*
- *250ml beef stock*
- *100ml red wine*
- *1 tbsp tomato puree*
- *400g can tomatoes*
- *400g can beans (cannellini or borlotti for example)*
- *1 tbsp redcurrant jelly parsley to garnish*

Serves 5-7

Method

- Add the oil and herbs to a large pan.
- Coat the beef with seasoned flour and brown in the pan.
- Transfer the beef to a slow cooker with a slotted spoon.
- Add the carrots, parsnip and onion to the pan and cook for about 5 minutes.
- Add the stock, wine, tomatoes, puree and jelly to the pan. Mix well and bring to the boil.
- Stir in the beans to the mixture and then transfer the contents of the pan to the slow cooker.
- Cook on high for about 1 1/2 hours and then on low for at least 6 hours.
- Spinkle with parsley.
- Great served with mashed potatoes and green vegetables.

  Freezes well.

A recipe that can be prepared in advance and then just left to cook slowly.

Very heartwarming on a cold winter's evening.

Bobotie

Helen Lomas - Former Scout Group Secretary

This is a traditional South African dish of my childhood. Perhaps Lord Baden-Powell ate this whilst serving in the Boer War.

Ingredients

- *1 thick slice of bread*
- *375 ml milk*
- *2 tbsp oil*
- *2 chopped onions*
- *2 crushed cloves of garlic*
- *5 tsp curry powder*
- *2 tsp salt*
- *2 tbsp mango chutney*
- *1 tbsp apricot jam*
- *1 tbsp Worcestershire sauce*
- *1 tsp turmeric*
- *5 tsp brown vinegar*
- *2 lb minced beef*
- *2 oz sultanas*
- *3 eggs*
- *2 bay leaves*

Method

- Soak the bread in the milk.
- Fry the onions and garlic.
- Add curry powder, salt, chutney, jam, Worcestershire sauce, turmeric and vinegar to frying pan.
- Drain milk from bread and mash bread. Retain milk.
- Add mince, bread and sultanas to frying pan.
- Fry slightly until meat browns.
- Put meat mix into large baking dish approx. 12" x 6".
- Mix eggs and leftover milk, pour over meat mix.
- Bake at 180°C for about an hour until egg mix is set.
- Serve with rice cooked with a pinch of turmeric and a handful of raisins.

Seared Turbot
with Celeriac Mash, Broad Beans and Peas and a Champagne and Shellfish Veloute

Rev Kate Bottley - Celebrity Masterchef 2017

Ingredients

For the veloute

- 30g butter
- 3 banana shallots
- 100g button mushrooms
- 150ml white wine
- 150ml champagne
- 150ml vermouth
- 500ml shellfish stock (made from shellfish, carrot, celery, parsley, white pepper, salt)
- 150g double cream
- 4 parsley stalks
- 1 sprig thyme
- 4 sprigs tarragon
- salt
- white pepper

For the Celeriac

- Whole celeriac
- Whole milk
- Pinch of nutmeg
- Seasoning
- Butter

For the veg

- Broad beans
- Fresh peas
- Mint
- Butter
- Seasoning

For the turbot

- 4 best turbot steaks (skin on but deboned)
- Rape seed oil
- Pea shoots to garnish

Method

For the Veloute

- Make the shellfish stock.
- On a medium heat, fry the fennel, shallots and garlic in the butter, and sweat without colouring.
- Add the mushrooms and continue to cook until the mushrooms have yielded their liquid and the pan is dry. Add the white wine, vermouth and reduce by at least 50%. Add the stock and reduce again. Add the cream, parsley and thyme. Simmer, season, remove from the heat and add the tarragon. Sieve.

For the celeriac

- Peel and chop the celeriac, put into a heavy based saucepan with enough whole milk to cover and a pinch of the nutmeg. Simmer until softened (careful the milk doesn't boil over). Blend the celeriac with a hand blender until smooth, and season.

For the veg

- After the fish has cooked, add the beans and peas to the pan and a little of the shellfish stock. Cover and simmer until tender, add a little butter and some mint to taste.

For the turbot

- Pan fry the turbot skin side down in a little rapeseed oil until the skin is crispy and the fish is 3/4 of the way through cooked, then flip for the final minute to finish.
- Serve on a white plate, quenelle of celeriac, turbot on top, broad beans and peas around and a little of the veloute.
- Garnish with fresh pea shoots.

Homemade Cornish Pastry

Wayne Sleep OBE - Dancer, Director and Choreographer

Ingredients

For shortcut pastry

- *225g self-raising flour*
- *115g lard*
- *Pinch of salt*
- *Water*

For the filling

- *225g beef skirt, cut into small cubes*
- *2 to 3 large potatoes*
- *1 piece turnip or swede*
- *1 onion, peeled and chopped*
- *Salt & pepper*

Method

- Sift flour together with the salt, rub in the fat, and mix to a flexible consistency with some water. Leave to rest for half an hour.
- Roll out half the pastry into round approximately 5 mm thick.
- Peel and slice the potatoes thinly into the centre of round, this will form a base for the rest of the filling.
- Slice the turnip over the potato thinly and then spread the beef on top.
- Add a small amount of onion, season with salt and pepper.
- Dampen the edge of the circle of pastry with water to help seal it. Bring together the edges to make a parcel with the filling in the centre.
- You should have a neat parcel with the filling in the centre – make the pastry tidy by crimping the edges. Fold over the edge to make it slightly thicker, then squeeze every 2cms making a pattern along the edge.
- Place the pastry on a piece of buttered parchment paper, make a small slit on top to let the steam out, brush the top with some milk, and put on a greased baking tray.
- Bake it in a pre-heated over at 200°C (gas mark 6) for 30 minutes, reduce the heat to 190°C (gas mark 5) and cook for another 30 minutes.

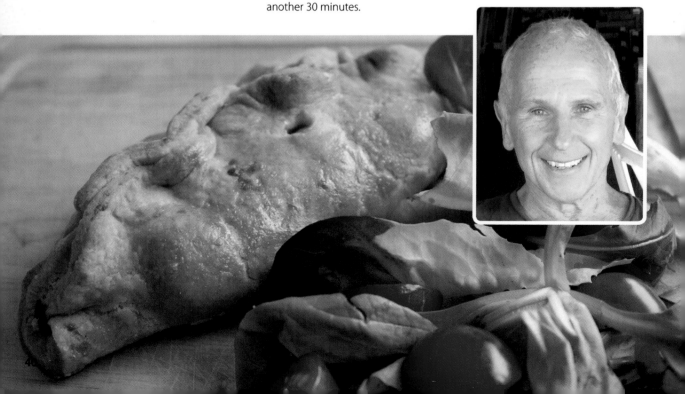

Fishy Finger Pie

Jenny & Mark Howard

Ingredients

- *Fish Fingers (good quality) - quantity dependant of the size of the oven-proof dish*
- *Potatoes (few good sized spuds for mash)*
- *Baked beans x 1 tin*
- *Mature cheese*

Method

- Peel and boil the potatoes until soft and ready to make mashed potato (you can add butter or milk as suited).
- Place Fish Fingers in a tray and cook in the over as per instructions.
- Warm baked beans in pan or Microwave.
- Grate cheese to add to the mashed potato for Cheesy Mash and save some for covering.
- Once components are ready, lay out the fish fingers in an oven-proof dish, add the baked beans over and around the Fish Fingers and then cover with the Cheesy Mash.
- Sprinkle the remaining grated cheese over the top and place in the oven at 180°C for a further 15 minutes or so until golden.
- Remove from the oven and enjoy this great combination.

Fish Pie

Sharron Davies MBE - Olympian

Ingredients

- *A pinch of salt and pepper*
- *100g of grated cheese*
- *100g of fresh prawns*
- *100g of scallops*
- *500g of potatoes*
- *2 fillets of fresh salmon*
- *250g of milk*
- *A spoon of butter*

Method

- Pre-heat your oven to 180°C. Peel & boil the potatoes until soft and then mash.
- Add a little butter and milk to the mash.
- Put the remaining butter and milk into a pan and heat.
- Add all fish to the remaining milk and butter and gently poach, breaking into small pieces. (This should take roughly 5 minutes) then add the seasonings, and 3/4 of the cheese.
- Put the fish and sauce into a dish and then layer on the mashed potato.
- Finally sprinkle on the remaining cheese and put into the oven for 15 minutes or until a golden brown colour on the top.

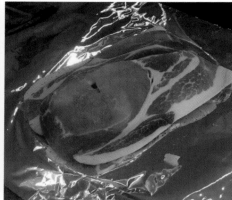

Cowboy Sandwiches

Charlie Howick - Explorer Scout Leader

Ingredients

- Bread - 2 slices
- Bacon - 4 rashers
- Baked beans
- Grated cheese
- Potato (optional)
- Mushroom (optional)
- Onion (optional)
- Aluminium foil

Method

- Start a fire and leave until you have a bed of hot embers.
- Lay out your tin foil and cut a piece out roughly 12 inches.
- Put down 2 rashers of bacon in the middle of the foil.
- Now add your fillings including beans, potato, mushroom and onion. Make sure you very thinly slice the potato to ensure it cooks properly. Once done put other slices of bacon back on top to seal fillings in.
- Fold foil over to form a parcel and place on the hot embers of the fire.
- Leave for around 10 minutes, depending on the heat of fire. Once you start to smell the bacon cooking take it out and check, if still not cooked place it back on, leave until the bacon is cooked to how you like it.
- Once cooked, unfold foil and place the bacon onto slice of bread. Sprinkle over the grated cheese and add any sauces you wish.
- Put another slice of bread on top and enjoy your cowboy sandwich!

My Name is Charlie Howick and I am one of the Explorer Scout leaders with 1st Gotham.

This is a recipe I use when teaching or practising bushcraft and is perfect over the fire!

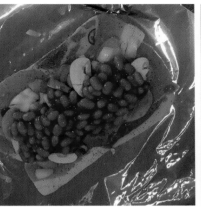

Underground Oven-Roasted Goat Legs

Ed Stafford - Explorer and Adventurer - Scout Ambassador

Ingredients

Allow:
- *1 leg per 3 people for a decent meal. (1 goat leg can be eaten by one person for a full day.)*
- *10 hours of your time (for a 6pm supper start at 8am)*
- *1 hour digging & prep.*
- *4 1/2hours fire.*
- *4 1/2 hours cooking.*
- *A spade or improvised digging tool*
- *About 20 rocks the size of apples (non-porous and not wet - they will explode!)*
- *Firewood (much more than you imagine)*
- *A lighter / matches / fire-by-friction set.*

Method

- Dig a hole the size of a big wok / dustbin lid in the ground (keeping the soil in a neat pile).
- Line the hole with the rocks as if they were cobbles (nice and close to each other) make a huge fire on top of the rocks.
- Allow to burn brightly and fiercely for 4.5 hours after which the fire should have died down enough to use a long stick to brush the embers neatly to the side. The rocks will be red hot so be careful. At night they could even glow white!
- Place your goat legs directly on the rocks (they will not burn I promise).
- Completely cover the legs in big broad green leaves like doc leaves in the UK. Coconut palm leaves work well if laid so that they cross each other at right angles.
- Cover the leaves with the remaining coals. Then cover the entire mound with the excavated soil.
- Leave for 4.5 hours to cook. Uncover carefully so as not to get soil on the meat.
- The legs (or whatever meat you choose to cook) will be so succulent and tender that you could bite it off with your lips - your toothless granny could do it! Enjoy.

Alternative

- Goat can be substituted for lamb, mutton, etc. I've used this method of cooking to make rats taste like a delicacy !

  You need NO SEASONING and cannot go wrong. This is one of the oldest and simplest forms of cooking ever.

This is a fantastic way to entertain if you are having a barbeque at the weekend and have the day to prepare. It will be so much tastier than anything cooked on the conventional barbecue.

I chose it because it also works in the wild when you have no cooking pot and want to roast meat.

On Olorua (an island where I survived for 60 days alone in the Discovery show Naked and Marooned) I hung the 4 cooked legs above the fire in the smoke to keep the flies off and ate one each day for 4 days.

> *I have swum, cycled and run the length of Britain and have always enjoyed spending time along our amazing shores. So much so that in 2016 I also travelled around Britain's entire coastline in the world's longest triathlon. I love being able to catch my own food. Not only does it taste better but it makes you understand a lot more about the food chain and where the food you buy in the supermarket comes from.*

Line Caught Mackerel on the Fire

Sean Conway - Scout Adventurer

Ingredients

- *1 mackerel fish, freshly caught*
- *Olive oil*
- *Salt*
- *Pepper*
- *Lemon*
- *1 large jacket potato*
- *Butter*

Method

This meal is more than just a meal, it's a life experience and I urge all children to try this once in their lives. This is what you need to do:

- Go down to the beach and find some driftwood that is 20-30 cm long. A 4 inch wide plank is best however a thick branch will do. Get rid of any excess bark and get a sharp knife and carve your own mark into the wood. You may want your name, your favourite animal or whatever means something to you. Carve it on the side, make it yours.

- Now cut some indents at the end of the wood so that you can tie the end of your fishing line to the plank so that it doesn't fall off.
  Good chance to use the knots you've learned to tie.

- Once the line is firmly attached start rolling the fishing line around the stick. You'll need about 20-30m of line.

- At the end of the line add 5 mackerel hooks and a heavy weight. Those who want to be more adventurous can make their own hooks with heavy duty wire and then use a rock as a weight but you don't have to.

- Now that you are ready to go head out in your canoe and drop the line and start paddling. This is the time to explore. You aren't just fishing, you are exploring the great British coastline. It may take some time to get a fish but keep at it. I once tied a line around my waist while I swam and it took me 3 hours of swimming to catch a fish. Be patient.

- You've finally caught a fish. Well done. Now head back to shore and build a fire somewhere safe.

- Wrap a potato in tin foil and put it in the coals early on. It may take half an hour to cook.

- Now gut the fish, add some olive oil, salt and pepper and put it on a grill over the fire. Wait 5 minutes and flip it over.

- Once it's cooked, plate it up with your baked potato. Add some lemon and butter and enjoy.

  There you have it. You have made your own rod, caught your own fish and cooked it. This is something you will remember forever.

Fillet of Beef with Prosciutto Ham and Wild Mushrooms

Phil Howick - Former Scout Group Chairman

Ingredients

- *900g good fillet beef*
- *150g mixture of fresh mushrooms (portabello & shiitake or any wild mushrooms)*
- *16 slices of prosciutto ham*
- *Fresh rosemary & thyme*
- *Large knob of butter*
- *Rapeseed oil*
- *Sea salt & pepper*
- *Some string to secure the ham*

Method

- Finely chop the mushrooms and the herbs.
- Fry the mushrooms using the rapeseed oil until cooked, add the chopped rosemary & thyme, butter, salt & pepper to taste. When cooked, leave to cool.
- On a piece of greaseproof paper place 3 or 4 pieces of string on the paper about 35mm apart before putting the ham on (makes it easier to tie up later).
- Lay the slices of prosciutto ham in a square, overlapping so that they form a sheet that will cover the fillet all over.
- When cool, put some of the mushrooms in the middle of the ham then place the fillet of beef on top, cover the beef with the rest of the mushrooms try to get an even cover. Then roll up the beef with the ham carefully but has tightly as you can, using the string to hold it all together. This can be done earlier in the day then put in the fridge.
- To cook, take out of fridge and let it warm to room temperature.
- Place on a roasting tray and put in a pre-heated oven heated at 200°c and cook for 30 to 40 mins.
- To check if cooked, use a temperature probe,
- For rare - the fillet needs to be 50°c. For medium-rare 56°c. For medium 60°c
- When cooked leave to rest on a carving board for about 15 minutes, cover with foil to keep warm, then slice. It should feed 4 people.

Enjoy.

Tomato Soup and Chips

Chris Howard - Mark's Dad

Ingredients

- A handful of potatoes suitable for chips
- Deep fat fryer/chip pan (please be careful with the hot oil)
- Vegetable oil
- Good quality tinned tomato soup

Method

- Peel and then briefly wash the potatoes to remove some starch.
- Slice the potatoes so they resemble chips.
- Place in fryer and cook until golden.
- Warm the tomato soup on the hob and allow to simmer, not boiling it.
- Once cooked, place the chips in the soup and reminisce.

Variation

- Add some grated mature cheese to the soup for a super mix!

My Dad would make this as his classic dish when I was growing up. It reminds me of being at home on a chilly night, enjoying the company of my mum and dad.

A simple, but amazing combination which means a great deal to me. I have submitted this recipe on my dad's behalf - Mark.

Mac 'n' Four Cheese

Andrew Bassford - Scout Group Chairman

Ingredients

- *450g macaroni*
- *200g diced pancetta*
- *1 shallot, chopped*
- *3 tbsp plain flour*
- *500ml milk*
- *250g grated Cheddar cheese*
- *125g grated Gruyere cheese*
- *125g finely chopped Mozzarella cheese*
- *Salt and pepper to taste*
- *120g panko breadcrumbs*
- *2 tbsp grated Parmesan cheese*
- *1 tbsp butter*

Method

- Preheat oven 175°C.
- Using a large saucepan of lightly salted boiling water, cook the pasta until al dente, or firm to the bite. Drain and set aside.
- Sauté pancetta in a large saucepan until browned thoroughly. Do not drain the fat.
- Add the chopped shallot, cooking until it is soft and golden.
- Stir the flour into the shallot and pancetta and cook for 1 minute.
- Add in the milk gradually, stirring continuously. Bring to a gentle boil, again stirring continuously.
- Set aside a dessert spoon of the Cheddar, Gruyere and Mozzarella cheeses.
- Gradually add the remaining grated cheeses, stirring while they melt into the sauce. When complete, remove the pan from the heat.
- Stir the pasta into the cheese mixture and then pour into a large baking dish.
- Stir the breadcrumbs, Parmesan and reserved cheeses together in a bowl; sprinkle over the top of the pasta mixture.
- Cut butter into small pieces and spread evenly over the top.
- Bake in the preheated oven until bubbly and golden, about 20 minutes.

Tasty and interesting twist on a standard recipe.
The four cheeses really lift the depth and complexity
of flavour above ordinary macaroni cheese, while
the pancetta is a great extra taste.
But this is still simple and quick to make.

Cowboy Casserole

Kathryn Wills - District Commissioner, Rushcliffe District Scouts

Ingredients

- *1 packet of smoked or unsmoked bacon*
  (chopped into small pieces after cooking)
- *1 pkt sausages*
  (chopped into small pieces after cooking)
- *1 large onion (chopped)*
- *1 pkt button mushrooms*
  (left whole or chopped depending on size)
- *1 tin baked beans*

Method

- Fry or grill the sausages and then chop into small pieces about 2cm long.
- Fry or grill the bacon and then chop into small pieces.
- Fry the onion and mushrooms.
- Put all of the above into one pan (you can use one pan from the beginning if you want to).
- Add the baked beans and warm through.

This was one of my favourite one pan meals for Cub camp and I still make it now.

Dishwasher Poached Salmon

Penny Gwynne

Ingredients

- *Whole side of salmon cleaned*
- *Juice of one lemon or bottled variety*
- *Olive oil*
- *Salt & pepper*
- *Large roll of extra strong foil*

I had heard of this recipe years ago in the catering circles and when I needed to cook salmon for 70. I looked up past ideas and made up the recipe here.

This produced a beautifully cooked and tasty poached salmon with very little effort.

Method

- Roll out a sheet of foil 20cm longer than the salmon.
- Sprinkle centre line of foil with a little lemon, oil and seasoning.
- Wipe salmon and place skin down on centre line, sprinkle lemon, oil and seasoning on the upward facing flesh.
- Draw sides of the foil together over the salmon and make a double fold (pleat) to seal.
- Roll up ends and seal in a similar way.
- Lay out the second sheet of foil and wrap the foiled salmon again.
- Place wrapped salmon in the top rack of the dishwasher (front to back).
- Start the dishwasher on a 6 degree cycle and allow cycle to complete uninterrupted (and without the detergent tablet)!
- Remove wrapped salmon, uncover and refrigerate before using.

Dan & Brodie's Baked Bean Slop

Dan (Scout Leader) and Brodie (Cub Scout)

Ingredients

- 1 x 410g tin of baked beans
- 1 x 160g tin of tuna, drained
- 1 x 198g tin of sweetcorn, drained
- 70g cheddar cheese cut into cubes

Method

- Add the drained tuna to a large saucepan on a medium heat.
- Stir for 1 minute to remove any excess liquid.
- Add the beans and sweetcorn.
- Leave on heat for 3 minutes stirring occasionally.
- Turn the heat down to low and add the cheese cubes.
- After a couple of minutes the cheese will start to melt. Remove from the heat and serve.
- Serve with thick cut white toast or on a wrap.

Sausage Fajitas

Dan and Brodie

Ingredients

- 1 pack of 8 sausages
- 1 onion
- 150g sweetcorn
- 1 red pepper
- 1 yellow pepper
- Tomato puree tube
- 1 tsp of paprika
- 1 tsp of cumin
- 1/2 tsp of cayenne pepper
- 2 garlic cloves
- Salt & pepper

To Serve

- Wraps
- Lettuce
- Sour cream
- Red jalapeños
- Grated cheddar

Makes 8 fajitas

Method

- Chop the peppers and onion into chunky strips.
- In a large wok, gently fry the sausages until lightly browned on a medium heat.
- Cut each sausage with scissors into 4 or 5 pieces.
- Add the onion and pepper to the wok and crush the garlic into the wok and stir together.
- Add the sweetcorn. Cook for 1 minute.
- Add a good squeeze of the tomato puree, the paprika and cumin and stir.
- Add the cayenne pepper. If you don't like spice leave it out or add more for a livelier dish.
- Add a good pinch of salt and pepper and stir. Turn the heat down to low. Cook for 5 minutes stirring occasionally.
- Heat 2 wraps per person in a microwave for 20 seconds.
- Remove the sausage and vegetables from the heat and pour into a large bowl.
- Spread a large dollop of the mix into a wrap and top with the grated cheese, lettuce, sour cream and jalapeños.

  Roll the wrap and eat!

Post Match Lasagne

Chris & Cherry O'Grady

Ingredients

- 1 box of lasagne pasta sheets
- 1 cooking onion
- 1 crushed garlic clove (or pre-chopped garlic)
- Mixed herbs
- 4 beef stock cubes (the dry type)
- 1 small tin of tomato puree
- 4 tins chopped/plum tomatoes
- 1 jar lasagne tomato sauce
- 1 block of mozzarella
- 1 small tub of mascarpone
- 1 block of parmesan cheese

- Around 700g lean beef mince meat (lamb or veg option)
- You will also need a deep pan for your sauce, a frying pan to prep your meat and a large square dish to prep and then cook your lasagne in.

Method

1 - Making the sauce

- Fry half of a chopped onion in a deep pan.
- Add 4 tins of chopped tomatoes once onions have softened (keep simmering).
- Add one jar of lasagne tomato sauce (flavoured with garlic/spices/wine if preferred).
- Add one small tin of tomato puree.
- During cooking add a splash of salt, pepper, half a tea spoon of sugar, mixed herbs and lastly crush half of a garlic clove (if preferred use pre-chopped garlic, it is lazy but it's garlic).
- Once warmed, blend the sauce together using a potato masher to create a smooth finish.
- Leave to simmer whilst moving on to preparing step 2.
  (there will be plenty of sauce left over after step 3, this is to reheat once the lasagne is cooked and to be poured over the lasagna).

2 - The meat

- Fry the other half of the chopped onion in a deep frying pan.
- Add around 700g of lean mince beef meat (lamb or veg alternative if preferred).
- Add salt, pepper, mixed herbs and more garlic.
- Add 4 beef stock cubes crumbled over for extra flavour.
- Leave to simmer whilst moving on to the final step 3.

  Preparing to put your lasagne together you'll need to slice your mozzarella block into around 16 slices. Have your mascarpone and lasagna ready to go.

After a 90 minute football Match nothing goes down better in the O'Grady household than our family recipe lasagne.

Made by Chris O'Gradys partner Cherry who was taught by her father Malcolm Waddilove. Malcolm followed the recipe from his mother who married an Italian American in New York.

This recipe originates from a true Italian and is certainly worth trying as its like no other!

3 - Layering the lasagne

- Pour half of your meat into your square dish. Add a few splashes of your sauce to help keep the meat moist.
- Now add your first layer of lasagne sheets over the meat, only one layer needed.
- Next add around 8 slices of mozzarella.
- Now add your second layer of lasagne sheets.
- Next pour in the rest of your meat (again add a splash of sauce).
- Now add a third layer of lasagne sheets.
- Next add the remaining slices of mozzarella, now for the messy part. Spread the mascarpone over the mozzarella mixed with a splash of sauce to make it easier to spread.
- Add your final layer of lasagne sheets.
- Lastly add a final layer of sauce over the final layer of sheets, sprinkle Parmesan cheese and a pinch of mixed herbs to finish off.
- Once the lasagne has been put together cover in foil, prick it and cook in a fan oven on 180°C for an hour and 20 mins.
- For that last 20 minutes remove foil.
- Reheat the rest of the sauce once cooked and pour over the lasagna to add that extra flavour. Best served with a simple salad and garlic bread!

Enjoy!!!

Glamping
Puddings / Desserts

Chocolate Delight

Selasi Gbormittah - GBBO 2016

Ingredients

The Cake

- *85g unsalted butter*
- *160g caster sugar*
- *1 tsp vanilla bean paste*
- *2 large egg, beaten separately*
- *210g plain flour sifted*
- *50g cocoa powder*
- *3 tsp teaspoon baking powder*
- *245ml whole milk.*

To decorate

- *Punnet of strawberries, raspberries, black berries, cherries (Or your favourite fruits), chopped*
- *300ml double cream*
- *1 1/2 tbsp icing sugar, sifted*
- *3-4 tbsp cocoa powder, sifted*
- *3-4 tbsp cherry or blackcurrant jam*

Dusting

- *1 tbsp icing sugar*

Method

- Pre heat the oven at 180°C (fan ove n).
- In your mixer, whisk the butter, sugar and vanilla until light and fluffy.
- Add the beaten egg and mix for 1 minute on low speed.
- Add the remaining ingredients and mix gently until fully incorporated (ideally fold).
- Line two 8-9 inch sandwich tins with butter and greaseproof paper.
- Equally divide the mix into each tin and bake for 18-20 minutes.
  Stick a cocktail stick into cake after 20 minutes to make sure it is baked. If not, bake for a further 3-5 minutes.
- Cool on a cooling rack.
- Make filling by first whipping the cream on medium to high speed.
  Be careful not to over whip. Should form stiff peaks at 4-5 minutes.
  Add the icing sugar and cocoa powder gradually and fold in until well mixed.
- To assemble, place one layer of cooled cake onto a plate/cake board and spread with half the jam. Gently pipe or spread cream onto jam evenly. Top with your mixed fruits.
- Place your second layer of cake onto the first and repeat previous step.
- Dust with a tbsp of icing sugar and serve.
  Try not to share!

Fruit Cake in an Orange

Mark Howard

Ingredients

This makes around 6 - 10 fruit cakes (depending on the size of the orange) -

- *1 orange per cake*
- *100g caster sugar*
- *110g butter (unsalted)*
- *2 eggs*
- *110g plain flour*
- *2 tsp baking powder*
- *1 tsp ground cinnamon*
- *1 tsp ground nutmeg*
- *120g raisins*
- *25g glacé cherries (quartered)*

(Other options can include chocolate chips, sultanas etc.)

Method

This recipe is traditionally cooked on campfire embers for a good 40 to 50 minutes. Alternatively an oven can be used, cooking time around 40 minutes.

Preparation

- Preheat oven to 180°C (fan assisted) or prepare campfire and allow for a good bed of embers for cooking (if using a campfire please use with caution).
- Begin by removing the top of the orange, slice about 1cm down from the top. You will still need to keep the top of the orange.
- Remove the inner of the orange with a spoon, making this hollow but leaving the skin intact.

Mixture

- Using the softened butter and caster sugar, mix until fluffy.
- Then, beat in the eggs (one at a time).
- Add the flour and baking powder and continue to mix to a smooth texture.
- Add the cinnamon and nutmeg and mix.
- Add the raisins and cherries (or alternative) and mix.
- Once the above is complete, half fill the oranges with the mixture, replace the top of the orange and wrap firmly in foil.
- Place in oven and leave for a good 50 minutes until cooked.
- Remove foil carefully; cooling slightly and eating warm.

  The cake may at times seem a bit soggy but this can be due to the orange moisture.

As a big fan of the great outdoors, I would normally cook these with friends or family and the local Scout Group where I am a leader. It's a great way for young people to try some unique cooking by using an orange instead of a cake mould.

This is one of my favourite recipes for campfire cooking. However, cooking on a campfire is not always possible, so it's good to bring the outside in. This still works well in an oven and the concept of cooking in a orange just brings something different to the kitchen.

Blackberry Bakewell Tarts

Andrew Smyth - GBBO 2016

Ingredients

- *375 g pack shortcrust pastry (ready rolled)*
- *100 g unsalted butter, at room temperature*
- *100 g caster sugar*
- *1 large free-range egg*
- *1/2 tsp almond extract*
- *100 g ground almonds*
- *15 g plain flour*
- *140 g blackberries (~ 50 blackberries)*
- *30 g flaked almonds*
- *40 g icing sugar*
- *1/4 tsp almond extract*
- *Double cream, to serve (optional)*

Makes 12 individual tarts
45 mins total time

Method

- Preheat the oven to 200C / fan 180°C. Make sure you've got a 12-hole muffin tin and a 9 cm circular cutter or something that size to cut around.

- Bring the pastry to room temperature then unroll onto a very lightly floured surface. Use a 9 cm cutter to cut out circles and press them gently into the muffin tin. Chill in the fridge while you make the filling.

- In a large bowl, beat together the butter and caster sugar for about 5 minutes until pale and fluffy. Add the egg and 1/2 tsp almond extract and beat until well combined. Sieve in the ground almonds and flour then fold to incorporate.

- Dollop a tablespoon of the mix into each chilled pastry case and level off with a spoon. Press 4 blackberries into each case and sprinkle a few flaked almonds over.

- Bake in the middle shelf for 15-20 minutes until lightly golden brown. Remove from the tins carefully and leave to cool on a wire rack

- For the icing drizzle, mix the icing sugar with 1/4 tsp almond extract and a teaspoon or two of water and mix until thick and smooth.
Drizzle over the bakewells.

Serve with double cream.

The start of Autumn is the perfect time for foraging as blackberries come into season in a hedgerow near you. I've always been a bakewell tart fan (more so than the traditional pudding!) so a blackberry version really hits the spot for me. I also chose this recipe as a nod to a the county of Derbyshire which showed me such fantastic support on my journey to the final of The Great British Bake Off.

More recipes and updates of what I'm up to now are available on my website at
www.cakesmyth.com

Ice Cream & Fromage Frais
with variations

Jo Brand - Comedian, Writer and Actress

Ingredients

- *A big tub of ice cream might be upmarket or down (from a generic supermarket)*
- *Little tubs of chocolate fromage frais (as above)*

Method

- Dollop out or carefully spoon into individual bowls a fairly generous portion of ice cream.
- Spoon out, onto the ice cream the contents of the little tub of chocolate fromage.

And that's it!

Variations

- Add some fresh, peeled and roughly cut up pears.
  (A sort of Pear Helene - oops - copyright…)
- Fruit flavoured fromage frais.
  (Haven't tried it but might be a healthy option?)
- Fruit yogurt is also quite tolerable on icecream - it sort of freezes - and then you could add some blueberries or any sort of berry?
  Give it a go?
- Create the original and grate some milk chocolate on the top - Mmmm…

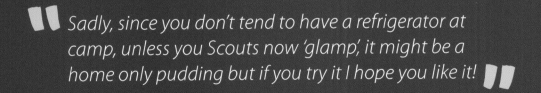

Sadly, since you don't tend to have a refrigerator at camp, unless you Scouts now 'glamp', it might be a home only pudding but if you try it I hope you like it!

Blueberry and White Chocolate Shortbread

Mary Howick

Ingredients

- 100g plain flour
- 50g semolina
- 100g softened butter
- 50g caster sugar
- 50g dried blueberries
- 50g white chocolate chips

Method

- Preheat oven to 150°C. Grease 6" round tin.
- Mix flour and semolina in bowl then rub in the butter. Stir in sugar and blueberries. Squeeze together into a ball.
- Press into tin. Chill for 30 mins then bake in the oven for about 40 mins.
- Mark and sprinkle with caster sugar.

Pete's Mom's Banana Bread

Judy and Pete Nelson - Treehouse Masters

Ingredients

- 3 large, ripe bananas
- 1 egg, well beaten
- 1 cup sugar
- 3 tbsp butter, melted
- 2 cups flour
- 1 tsp baking soda
- 1 tsp baking powder
- 1/2 tsp salt

Method

- Mash bananas well and mix with beaten egg.
- Add sugar and mix thoroughly then add melted butter.
- Sift together the remaining dry ingredients then add to banana mixture.
- Pour into a greased 5" x 9" loaf pan (or two smaller pans).
- Bake at 350°F for 50-60 mins (less if using two smaller pans).

This recipe is simple and easy and delicious. It's perfect for the Treehouse Master!
Judy Nelson

Limoncello and Plum Tart
TORTA ALLIMONCELLO

Gino D'Acampo - Chef

Image © Matt Russell

Ingredients

- *Zest and juice of 2 unwaxed lemons*
- *4 tbsp double cream*
- *100g ground almonds*
- *200g caster sugar*
- *5 medium eggs*
- *120g butter, melted*
- *10 tbsp Limoncello liqueur*
- *6 plums, cut into wedges*
- *Icing sugar, for dusting*

For the pastry

- *190g plain flour, plus extra for dusting*
- *100g chilled, unsalted butter, plus extra for greasing*

Method

- To make the pastry, sift the flour into a large bowl and use your fingertips to rub in the butter until the mixture resembles breadcrumbs.
- Add 2–3 tablespoons of cold water and mix to a dough.
- Bring together into a ball, wrap in clingfilm and chill for 20 minutes.
- Roll out the pastry on a floured surface to fit a 25cm loose-based flan tin. Grease the tin with a little butter, then line it with the pastry. Leave to rest in the fridge for at least 2 hours.
- Preheat the oven to 180°C / 350°F / gas mark 4. Line the pastry with greaseproof paper, fill with baking beans and bake blind for 15 minutes.
- Remove from the oven and leave to cool before removing the beans and paper.
- Put the lemon zest and juice in a large bowl. Add the cream, almonds, sugar, eggs and butter and mix together to a smooth paste using a hand blender. Stir in the Limoncello.
- Arrange the plums on the base of the pastry case and pour the lemon mixture on top.
- Bake in the centre of the oven for 20 minutes. Turn off the oven and leave the tart to cool in the oven.
- To serve, decorate with a thick layer of icing sugar.

" *This recipe comes from the beautiful town of Sorrento where Limoncello is used in nearly every dessert. In the south of Italy, we serve it after a big meal as a digestive served in a cold shot glass.*

If you don't fancy making the shortcrust pastry, feel free to use ready made – no one will know! "

From: Fantastico! by Gino D'Acampo. Published by Kyle Books.
Priced £14.99. Photography by Kate Whitaker

Lemon Tart

Jayne Torvill - Olympian

Ingredients

- *6 oz digestive biscuits*
- *2 oz butter*
- *juice and rind of 2 lemons*
- *1 can condensed milk*
- *1/2 pint double cream*

Method

Base

- Melt the butter, crush the biscuits and mix.
- Line a tin with mixture.

Filling

- Mix the juice and rind of 2 lemons, 1 can condensed milk and 1/2 pint double cream and pour into base.
- Chill in the fridge.
  Serve.

Big Mama's Jamaican Rum Cake

Alison Hammond - TV Personality

Ingredients

- *120g brown dark sugar*
- *120g butter*
- *2 eggs*
- *120g self raising flour*
- *100ml white rum*
- *100g mixed fruits*

Method

- Cover fruit in rum and leave for 3 days until absorbed. Preheat oven to 180°C.
- Beat butter and sugar together until fluffy, add eggs one at a time and mix until combined. Fold in rum, fruits and flour.
- Pour into a greased tin and bake for 40 minutes until golden and cooked through.
- Serve with custard.

Melk Tart

Helen Lomas

Ingredients

- *1 packet of flaky pastry*
- *2 tbsp plain flour*
- *4 tbsp sugar*
- *500ml milk*
- *2 eggs*
- *1 tsp grated orange peel*
- *Pinch of salt*

Method

- Line a flan dish with flaky pastry.
- Combine flour and sugar with a little milk.
- Boil the remaining milk.
- Add flour mixture to boiled milk.
- Boil for a further 3 mins.
- Allow to cool slightly and add egg yolks and salt.
- Fold in beaten egg whites and grated orange peel.
- Pour into flan dish and bake for 20 mins at 200°C.

Gluten Free Banana Loaf

Stacey Curzon – Explorer Scout Leader

Ingredients

- 140g butter, softened, plus extra for the tin
- 140g caster sugar
- 2 medium eggs, beaten
- 140g self-raising flour (gluten free)
- 1 tsp baking powder (gluten free)
- 3 small, very ripe bananas, mashed
- 50g icing sugar

Method

- Heat oven to 180°C/160°C fan/gas 4.
- Butter a 2lb loaf tin and line the base and sides with baking parchment.
- Cream the butter and sugar until light and fluffy, then slowly add the eggs with a little flour. Fold in the remaining flour, baking powder and bananas.
- Pour into the tin and bake for about 30 mins until a skewer comes out clean. Cool in the tin for 10 mins, then remove to a wire rack.
- Mix the icing sugar with 2-3 tsp water to make a runny icing. Drizzle the icing across the top of the cake to finish.

This recipe is really easy to make, doesn't create much mess and tastes delicious!

Perfect accompaniment to a nice cup of tea.

Orange and Lemon Posset

Penny Gwynne

Ingredients

- *Juice of 2 large satsumas or juice of 2 medium oranges*
- *Juice of half a lemon*
- *1 satsuma segmented for decoration*
- *55 g caster sugar*
- *300 ml double cream*

Looks good in 4-5 small wine glasses or tumblers

Method

- Mix juices and sugar in a 500ml jug and stir thoroughly.
- Carefully pour the cream into a small pan and heat gently until just boiling.
- Immediately pour hot cream over the juice mixture and stir.
- It will thicken slightly.
- Pour posset in to each glass or tumbler and chill at least 2 hours or overnight.
- Decorate with satsuma / orange segments.

This is a delicious, speedy and easy to make ahead dessert, which generally has folks licking the glass!

Lime Cheesecake

Mark Dennison

Ingredients

- *1 packet of ginger biscuits*
- *~50g butter*
- *2 tubs of mascarpone cheese*
- *Zest & juice of 2 limes*
- *Icing sugar*
- *Grated plain chocolate to decorate*

Method

- Melt the butter, bash packet of ginger biscuits (inside a plastic bag or 2!)… add butter and mould into bottom of a dish – this is the cheesecake base.
- Chill for 1-2 hours.
- Mix together mascarpone cheese, lime juice/zest and icing sugar (to taste)….. spoon over base and chill for 2 hours or more.
- Just before serving, grate (or shave, if you're fancy!) some plain chocolate over the top.

  Enjoy!

Jamboree
Treats

Cubs' Campfire Cones

Ben Anderson - Cub Scout Leader (Akela)

Ingredients

- Ice cream cones
- Aluminium foil

Filling options

- Marshmallows
- Chocolate buttons / Chocolate Spread
- Peanut butter
- Chopped bananas
- Apple slices
- Strawberries

Method

- Spread the peanut butter/chocolate spread on the inside of your cone, then fill it with the chocolate chips, mini marshmallows, banana slices or anything of your choice. It works best with marshmallows or chocolate as your base ingredient and then another ingredient(s) of your choice.
- Wrap the whole cone in tin foil and put on the hot grill or in your fire.
- Cook for about 5-10 minutes, turning occasionally.
- Peel back foil and enjoy.
- Be careful - don't burn yourself and always let an adult help!

This recipe is a quick and easy camp fire treat, which nearly everyone can enjoy because of how flexible it is. A firm fiery favourite, even if the banana slices are always left over at the end.

If you've got any left over bananas - you can make a slit down the centre of your banana, fill with chocolate buttons and wrap loosely in foil. Similarly place on the fire for 10 minutes.

Chocolate Tray Fridge Bake

Lorena

Ingredients

- 250 g digestive biscuits
- 300 g milk chocolate
- 150 g golden syrup
- 100 g butter
- 75 g raisins
- Optional: apricots; cherries; marshmallows; Maltesers

Method

- Line 20cm square tin with cling film.
- Melt chocolate, syrup and butter over simmering water.
- Put biscuits in a bag and crush with a rolling pin.
- Stir all dry ingredients into melted chocolate mixture.
- Spoon into tin and press down.
- Leave to set in fridge.

It's a super yummy treat.

Brownies

Tim Kidd - UK Chief Commissioner, The Scout Association

Ingredients

- *250g unsalted butter*
- *450g granulated sugar*
- *1 tsp vanilla pod suspension*
- *4 large eggs*
- *130g plain flour*
- *1 tsp baking powder*
- *125g cocoa*
- *225g nuts*

Method

- Line a baking tin with parchment paper (avoid greaseproof paper if possible as it sticks to the brownies and is a pain to remove!).

- Heat oven to 180°C (160°C fan) or gas mark 4.

- Melt the butter in a large bowl in a microwave oven (I cover the top of the bowl with cling film as sometimes the butter explodes in the microwave!).

- Add the sugar, eggs and vanilla and mix well together.

- In a separate bowl mix the flour, baking powder and cocoa.

- Add the dry ingredients to the wet ingredients and mix well then add the nuts and mix.

- Pour/spoon into the tin and cook for about 20 - 30 minutes depending on how squidgy you want them and the depth of the mixture (this is a bit of trial and error – in my tins which are 19 cm square, I cook for 30 minutes and I use two tins). Check if cooked using a skewer that should come out nearly clean when ready. The brownies should rise a bit and a crust should form on top.

- Leave to cool in the tin for about 15 minutes before cutting them up otherwise they just make a bit of a mess.

- For gluten free brownies, replace the flour with ground almonds and quarter of a teaspoon of Xanthan gum.

I've chosen this recipe as it is one of my favourites and always goes down well!
I always make them gluten free and they come out much more gooey which I love.

Honey Buns

Stephen Fry - Comedian, Actor, Writer and Presenter

Ingredients

- *2 eggs*
- *75 g caster sugar*
- *1 tsp soft dark sugar*
- *Pinch salt*
- *90 g self-raising flour*
- *1 tsp baking powder*
- *90 g melted butter - cooled*
- *1 tbsp honey*

Method

- Whisk together the eggs and sugars.
- Fold in the sifted flour, baking powder and salt.
- Leave the mixture to rest for 30 minutes.
- Stir in the melted butter and honey.
- Bake in cases, approx. 25 minutes at gas 6, 180°C.

Mum's Gingerbread

Natalie LaTouche - Parent

Ingredients

- *2 oz margarine / butter*
- *1 cup sugar*
- *2 eggs*
- *2 cups self-raising flour*
- *2 tsp ginger powder*
- *1 cup black treacle*
- *1 cup boiling water*
- *1 tsp baking soda*

Method

- Cream margarine/butter and sugar together until light and fluffy.
- Mix together eggs, water and black treacle.
- Mix flour, ginger, baking soda together.
- Combine wet mix and dry mix together until smooth.
- Fold wet batter into the sugar and butter mix.
- Grease a loaf tin and add batter to the tin (the batter is quite wet).
- Bake for 1 hour at 180°C.
- Cool and serve with lashings of butter.

My mum and nan were not great cooks at all growing up but this gingerbread was something my great nannie had taught them.

It holds so many amazing memories for me. The smell of it baking and the eating.

Icing shown as
serving suggestion

Honey Buns

The Art of Marshmallow Toasting

Jenny Howard

Ingredients

- *Marshmallows*
- *Skewers*
- *Green tree twigs - peel the bark away and make to a point (Ash, Willow etc).*

Method

Layers

- Using a campfire, get a good bed of embers.
- Place marshmallow on the twig / skewer.
- Place over fire embers and rotate until golden!
- Move away from embers.
- Once cooler, remove the top layer and eat.
- With the remaining marshmallow repeat the above process, until marshmallow is too small to continue!

Standard

- Using a campfire, get a good bed of embers.
- Place marshmallow on the twig / skewer.
- Place over fire embers and rotate until golden!
- Once cooler, Eat!

Marshmallow Tray Bake

Jenny & Mark Howard

Ingredients

- *Marshmallows (standard size)*
- *Milk chocolate bars (dependant on size of the dish)*
- *Digestive biscuits x1 pack*

Method

- Take an oven-proof dish or tray and layer the bottom with the milk chocolate covering the base.

- Then, cover the milk chocolate base with marshmallows sat on top.

- Place in the middle of a pre-heated oven at 160°C (fan assisted) for around 15 minutes (until the chocolate has started to melt).

- Optional - if you want a more golden marshmallow top, place under the grill for a few minutes.

- Eat using the digestive biscuit as a spoon. Wonderful stuff!

I chose this recipe as I make these scones for village events. The car boot and the flower festival are our yearly events. I make about 100 for the flower festival and they all seem to go.

I get lovely comments about my scones so I'm sharing the recipe so you can enjoy them when you make them.

Ali's Scones

Alison Harrison - Parent

Ingredients

- *700g self-raising flour*
- *2 tsp salt*
- *4 tsp baking powder*
- *4 tbsp caster sugar*
- *150g Stork margarine*
- *12-14 fl oz milk*
- *Strawberry jam*
- *Double cream, whipped*

Method

- Preheat oven to 230°C or gas mark 8.
- Sift together the flour, salt and baking powder into a large bowl.
- Add the sugar and mix in.
- Add the margarine, rub into the mixture until it resembles breadcrumbs.
- Gradually add the milk to form a dough but not sticky.
- Knead the dough on a lightly floured surface until smooth.
- Roll out the dough to a good ½" thickness using a 2" round cutter.
- Arrange scones on trays and brush tops with milk.
- Bake in oven for 10-15 mins until well risen and lightly golden on top.
- When cool, fill with jam and cream. Yummy!

Healthier Flapjack

Julie Bailey - 1st Gotham Scout Group Exec Member

Ingredients

- *100g butter*
- *100g coconut oil*
- *150g dried cranberries*
- *1 tbsp ground cinnamon*
- *100ml maple syrup*
- *150ml honey*
- *400g rolled oats*

Method

- Place all ingredients (except oats) in a pan and heat until butter, coconut oil, syrup and honey have melted and cranberries have softened.
- Stir in rolled oats until they are completely covered with above mixture.
- Transfer mixture into an oven proof dish lined with greaseproof paper (approx 20 cm x 30c m).
- Press mixture down with back of spoon.
- Bake for 20-25 mins in the middle of the oven at 180°C.

Whilst trying to eat healthily, eating this flapjack has prevented snacking on biscuits and chocolate!

Crackin' Carrot and Raisin Cake

Jenny Howard

Ingredients

For the Sponge

- *225 g peeled and grated carrots,*
- *1 tbsp peeled and grated root ginger,*
- *40 ml buttermilk*
  (or 30 ml milk & 10 ml lemon juice)
- *2 medium eggs*
- *1 tsp vanilla essence*
- *175 ml vegetable oil*
- *210 g caster sugar*
- *250 g plain flour*
- *1 tsp baking powder*
- *1/2 tsp bicarbonate of soda*
- *1 tsp ground cinnamon*
- *1 tsp ground ginger*
- *1/2 tsp salt (optional)*
- *100 g raisins*

For the Frosting

- *50 g unsalted butter, softened*
- *300 g icing sugar*
- *2 tsp finely grated orange zest*
- *125 g full fat soft cheese*

Method

- Pre heat the oven to 170°C (fan assisted), and line 2 sandwich cake tins with baking parchment.
- Using a hand-held whisk, mix the carrots, root ginger, buttermilk, eggs, vanilla essence, vegetable oil and sugar together until they are well combined.
- Sift together the flour, baking powder, bicarbonate of soda, salt and ground spices. You then want to add them into the dry ingredients in 3 batches, mixing well each time, making sure to keep scraping down the sides of the bowl.
- Add in the raisins and mix until all thoroughly combined.
- Split the mixture between the 2 prepared tins and bake for approx. 30 mins, or until the top of the sponge bounces back when pressed lightly.
- Allow the cakes to cool completely on wire racks.
- Using a hand held whisk, mix the icing sugar and butter together on a low speed (it can be dusty) until combined but will still be a powdery consistency.
- Add the orange zest and cream cheese, increase the speed and mix well until it's fluffy, smooth and light.
- When the cake is cool, spread some of the frosting on top of one of the cakes. Place the other cake on the top and then repeat with the remaining frosting.

Pemmican Cake

Scott Heffield – Mountaineer and Adventurer

Ingredients

- 2 cups meat (Any biltong or jerky)
- 2 cups dried fruit
- 2 cups rendered fat
- Half a cup of mixed nuts (not essential)
- 1 good shot of honey

Method

- First, finely chop the dried meat and fruit.
- Crush your mixed nuts and place all in a small saucepan. Now add the rendered fat, beef suet is best.
- Slowly heat the mixture, stirring all the time until the fat has melted. Be careful not to boil the fat.
- Now add a good squirt or shot of honey in to the mix and stir in thoroughly.
- Finally, prepare a shallow baking tray and line with grease proof paper.
- Poor in the mix and spread evenly around the tray. Let the mix cool, wrap in the rest of the grease proof paper and store.
- The cake will keep and can be consumed for several years to come. Delicious!

" So, make no mistake about it, Pemmican is not really a delicious cake perfect for high teas. On the contrary, it is very much an acquired taste to say the least.

However, if you are on a mountain day, a long hike, on an adventure or in a survival situation, there is nothing better.

So, Pemmican has been around for a long time and was originally used by a variety of native tribes, worldwide. It likely originates from North America and was first made by the native Americans as a high-energy, highly nutritious, and filling food that would last for long periods of time. Later used by Arctic and Antarctic explorers such as Robert Falcon Scott (Scott of the Antarctic) and Shackleton.

This amazing stuff is a dried mixture of meat, berries and rendered fat (also called suet or tallow). It is an invaluable survival food that when prepared properly can last anywhere from several months to several years without refrigeration! "

Scott Heffield is a former Royal Marine Commando, a professional
mountaineer and adventurer who has worked and survived in some
of the most challenging environments on the planet. Working as
part of the Bear Gryll's safety team, Scott can be found alongside
Bear on TV shows such as Mission Survive or Survival School or
more commonly working with Bear behind the camera scouting new
locations and working as a safety supervisor and as crew safety on
shows such as NBC's Running Wild and ITV's, Bear's mission with…
He is also the lead instructor on the Bear Gryll's Survival Academy
running courses for families throughout the UK.

Jenny's Muddy Roads!

Jenny Howard

Ingredients

- 170g soft butter
- 400g dark choc
- 4 tbsp golden syrup
- 200g rich tea biscuits
- 100g digestive biscuits
- 125g mini marshmallows
- 2 x small bags maltesers
- 30g raisins

Method

- Melt the butter, golden syrup and chocolate in a saucepan. Tip out around 1/4 of the mixture once melted and leave to on side (this is for the top).
- Put both types of biscuits a in strong bag (sandwich or freezer bags work well) and then bash with a rolling pin until you've got a mixture of crumbs and small pieces.
- Add the biscuit bits into the chocolate mixture, then add the marshmallow, maltesers and raisins and mix until combined.
- Line a baking tin with foil making sure it comes up and slightly over the top (I find this easier to get it out by pulling on the foil).
- Tip in the mixture and flatten with the back of a spoon. Pour over the chocolate mixture smoothly to make a neat finish.
- Place in the fridge to set, around 2 hours or overnight.
- When set take out tray and cut into the sizes you'd like! Enjoy!

Jewish Ginger Cake

Darren Altman - Impressionist - Britain's Got Talent

Ingredients

- *8oz self raising flour 6oz sugar*
- *3 tbsp syrup*
- *3 tsp dry ginger*
- *2 tsp cinnamon*
- *2 eggs*
- *1 cup of warm water*
- *1 tsp bicarbonate of soda*
- *1 cup of vegetable oil*

Method

- Simply mix all the ingredients together in a bowl (don't worry that the mixture is runny!).
- Pour into a greased tin.
- Bake for 1 hour 15 minutes on gas mark 3. Fan oven 150° C.
- Tastes lovely warm, but if you can bear to leave it for a day, it goes gooey and tastes even better!

This recipe is one that my wife introduced me to, as her mother has been making it for her since she was a small girl.

It was given to her by a Jewish friend over 40 years ago.

Simple and Quick Brownie Recipe!

Elizabeth - 1st Gotham Explorer Scout

Ingredients

- *300g caster sugar*
- *110g butter (melted)*
- *30g cocoa powder*
- *1 tsp vanilla extract*
- *2 eggs*
- *110g plain flour*
- *Tiny bit of baking powder*
- *Add handful of chocolate chips if wanted*

Method

- Mix all ingredients together.
- Bake in oven at 180°C / gas mark 4 for 20-25 minutes.

Matt's Candy Cookies

Matthew - 1st Gotham Scout

Ingredients

- *200g plain flour, sifted*
- *50g milk chocolate chips (optional)*
- *1/2 tsp baking powder*
- *1/2 tsp bicarbonate of soda*
- *1/2 tsp salt*
- *125g candy coated sweets (Smarties)*
- *75g unsalted butter*
- *50g light soft brown sugar*
- *1 large egg, beaten*

Method

- Preheat oven to 180°C or gas mark 4.
- Grease baking trays.
- In mixing bowl, combine the flour, chocolate chips, baking powder, bicarbonate of soda, salt and half the sweets.
- In a separate bowl, beat together the butter and sugar using an electric whisk until light and fluffy.
- Gradually add the beaten egg, whisking it in.
- Fold in the flour mixture until all mixed in, using your hands.
- Refrigerate the dough for 20 mins.
- Taking a small handful of dough, roll into balls (approx. 12). Place on baking trays spaced apart.
- Flatten each ball a little and stud with the remaining candy sweets.
- Place in oven and bake for 10-12 mins until just set.
- Remove from the oven and allow to rest on the trays for 5 mins before removing onto a wire rack.

Mary's Special Fudge Squares

Mary Howick

Ingredients

- 125g butter
- 2 tbsp golden syrup
- 250g crushed digestive biscuits
- 50g raisins
- 25g cherries, chopped
- 150g plain chocolate, chopped

Fudge Icing

- 50g plain chocolate
- 25g butter
- 3 dsp water
- 175g icing sugar

Method

- Grease and line a 6" square tin.
- Put butter, syrup and chocolate in a pan and melt gently. Stir in biscuits, raisins and cherries.
- Press into tin and chill in the fridge.

Fudge Icing

- Melt chocolate, butter and water in a bowl over a pan of hot water. Remove from the heat when melted. Stir in icing sugar and beat until thick.
- Spread fudge icing over cake and chill again.
- Turn out of tin, sprinkle with icing sugar and cut into small squares.

Where's my Woggle?

Drinks

Sloe / Damson / Rhubarb / Gooseberry Gin

Julie Bailey - 1st Gotham Scout Exec member

Ingredients

- Fruit (approx. 1/3 of container that you are using)
- Gin (approx. 1 litre)
- 4-6oz Sugar (depending on how sweet you like it)
- If using rhubarb, the pinker the better as it colours the gin.

Method

- Sterilise a kilner type preserving jar or bottle (I pour boiling water into a jar/bottle to do this so make sure it is heat proof).
- Place chosen fruit into jar/bottle until 1/3 full. If using damson or sloe, wash/freeze fruit first as this will mimic a frost splitting the fruit skins and negating the need to prick them.
- Using a funnel, put in the desired amount of sugar depending on sweetness (you can always add more later).
- Add gin using the funnel, leave enough space at the top for the mixture to move around when you turn it.
- Place lid on jar/bottle and gently shake/turn until sugar is dissolved.
- Store in a cool, dark, dry place.
- For the first two weeks, turn/shake every other day, then once a week.
- For best results for sloe/gooseberry/damson, the longer the fruit is in, the better the results. However, if you pick in September, it will be ready for Christmas. For rhubarb, strain mixture through a piece of muslin after 2 months.
- Either drink neat or with tonic water.

Sam's Super Smoothie

Sam Howard

Ingredients

- *5 tbsp natural yoghurt*
- *150ml milk*
- *1 medium sized banana*
- *10 frozen cherries*
- *5 frozen strawberries*
- *1 Tsp of chocolate spread*
- *Based on 600ml bottle*

Method

- Using a blender place the banana, frozen strawberries, frozen cherries, in the blender's bottle/glass/jug. Add the natural yoghurt and milk, then the teaspoon of chocolate spread.
- Blend until smooth, pour and enjoy the cool freshness.

Sam says: **"** *It's yummy!* **"**

Fancy Hot Chocolate with Chocolate

Mark Howard

Ingredients

- *Water based hot chocolate powder (I normally used the lower/lighter sugar version)*
- *Good quality milk chocolate bar*
- *Mini marshmallows*
- *Squirty cream*
- *Hot water*

Method

- Add hot chocolate powder to mug (follow container guidelines for number of spoons).
- Add a little milk to the powder and stir to make a paste.
- Add a couple of chunks of milk chocolate.
- Pour in hot water from kettle (pan, storm kettle etc.) but leaving space at the top and stir.
- Add squirty cream and mini-marshmallows and enjoy.

" *Great to warm up on a cold winter's night or when around the campfire.* **"**

'Brack' to Basics

Retro

The following recipes first appeared in *The Gotham Recipe Book* produced in 1979 as a fundraiser for 1st Gotham Scout Group.

Gotham Special

Molly

Ingredients
- 8 ozs of short crust pastry for tartlet cases (or plate pie)

Filling
- 4 ozs sausage meat
- 4 ozs minced cooked liver (liver sausage may be used instead)
- Tsp of chopped onion
- Pinch of mixed herbs
- 1/2 oz Butter or margarine
- 2 tablespoons of stock
- Pepper & salt to taste

Method
- Heat fat in a pan - fry onion gently - add sausage meat - minced liver.
- Fry gently at moderate heat stirring until heated through - add stock - herbs and seasoning.
- Stir well until mixture forms a soft paste.
- Put spoonful of mixture in pastry base and cover with lid.
- Bake at about 420°F for about 12 minutes.

Scout Jubilee Special

Sybil

Ingredients
- Slice of toast buttered
- Slice of ham
- Poached egg
- Grated cheese

Method
- Slice of toast buttered
- Add a slice of ham, a lightly toasted poached egg, sprinkle with grated cheese and replace under the grill for half a minute.

Summer Chicken Pie

Sheila

Ingredients

Pastry

- 8 oz plain flour
- 2 oz lard and 2 oz margarine
- 6 to 7 teaspoonful cold water
- 1 teaspoon salt

Filling

- 2 eggs
- 1 teaspoon dried tarragon or half teaspoon sweet herbs
- salt and pepper
- 1/4 pint of milk
- grated rind ½ lemon
- 2 1/2 lb chicken roasted, skinned & taken off bone or 1 lb cold cooked chicken.

Method

- Sift together flour and salt. rub in fat, bind with water and leave to rest 10 mins

- Blend egg and milk in large bowl, add tarragon or herbs, lemon rind, salt and pepper. stir in chicken cut into 1/2" strips.

- Roll out 2/3rds of pastry to line 7" flan tin, leaving 1/4 overlapping. Fill with mixture. Dampen edges.

- Roll out remaining 1/3rd pastry to 8" circle and cover pie. Seal edges and trim to ¼"overlap, then flute & raise.

- Make 6 slits each about 1" long all from centre of pie. Damp centre and roll back points to make a star shape.

- Bake in hot oven 20 mins. Then remove flan ring carefully and bake for 40 mins. more at moderate temperature.

Brack

Olive

Ingredients

- 2 cups self raising flour
- 1 cup brown sugar (soft)
- 3/4 lb mixed dried fruit
- 1 egg (well beaten)
- 1 cup cold tea

Method

- Soak overnight fruit and sugar in tea.

- Next day add flour and egg. Mix well and pour into 1 lb. loaf tin.

- Bake for 2 hours at 300o (Reg, 3).

- Keep at least 1 day.

- Slice and butter.

Apricot Nectar Cheesecake

Mary

Ingredients

Base

- 5 oz plain sweet biscuits
- 2 1/2 oz butter

Filling

- 15 oz can apricot nectar
- 12 oz packaged cream cheese
- 1 tablespoon lemon juice
- 1 tablspoon gelatine
- 1/2 cup caster sugar
- 1/2 pt. cream

Topping

- 1 tablespoon. sugar
- 1 1/2 dsp arrowroot
- 1 dessertspoon rum (if liked)

Method

Base

- Combine bicuit crumbs and melted butter, mix well. Press mixture firmly on to a base of 8" springform pan - refrigerate for 1 hour.

Filling

- Measure 1 cup apricot nectar from can (save remainder for topping). Pour nectar into small saucepan, sprinkle gelatine over. place over low heat and stir until gelatine is dissolved, allow to cool and thicken slightly.

- Beat cream cheese and sugar until smooth, add lemon juice. Beat in apricot mixture then fold in whipped cream. Pour mixture on to crumb base - refrigerate 2 hrs or until firm.

Topping

- Place sugar and arrowroot in saucepan - gradually stir in reserved apricots. Bring to boil, stirring constantly, remove from heat - add rum.

- Allow to cool - spread over cheesecake, return to refrigerator for 1 hour.

Refrigerator Biscuits
(Ice Box Cookies)

Teresa

Ingredients

- 8 oz plain flour
- 6 oz caster sugar
- 1 level tsp baking powder
- 1 teaspoon vanilla essence
- 4 oz butter
- 1 beaten egg

The dough is rich and soft and needs to be chilled in the fridge before use. Keep a long roll wrapped in foil and cut off rounds to make biscuits as needed:

Method

- Rub the butter into the flour and baking powder until the mixture is like fine crumbs. Add the sugar and mix to a dough with the egg. Lay the mixture onto a long strip of aluminum foil and shape it into a sausage about 2" diameter.

- Wrap the foil around and twist the ends. Chill overnight. This will make 4 to 5 dozen thin biscuits as required. Slice thinly and lay them on a buttered tray well apart.

- Bake in the middle of a fairly hot oven (375F Mark 5) until they are golden (10mins). Use as much of the roll as required and return the rest to the fridge.

Syllabub

Anne

Ingredients

- Juice of 1 large lemon
- 2 tablespoons brandy
- 1/2 pint double cream
- 4 tabespoons sweet sherry
- 2 oz caster sugar

Method

- Put all liquids in a bowl.

- Add sugar and dissolve.

- Add cream. Whisk until thick.

- For a non-alcoholic syllabub, replace sherry and brandy with fresh orange juice.

Useful Stuff

Temperature conversions

Fahrenheit	Celsius	Gas Mark	Terminology
200°F	100°C		
225°F	110°C	1/4	Very Cool or Very Slow
250°F	120°C	1/2	Very Cool or Very Slow
275°F	140°C	1	Very Cool or Very Slow
300°F	150°C	2	Cool or Slow
325°F	160°C	3	Warm
350°F	180°C	4	Moderate
375°F	190°C	5	Moderate
400°F	200°C	6	Moderately Hot
425°F	220°C	7	Hot
450°F	230°C	8	Hot
475°F	240°C	9	Hot
500°F	260°C	10	Very Hot

Weights

Metric	Approx Imp Equiv
10-15g	1/2 oz
25g	1 oz
50g	2 oz
75g	3 oz
100-125g	4 oz
150-175g	6 oz
200-250g	8 ox
300-375g	12 oz
400-500g	1 lb
600-750g	1 1/2 lb
800-1000g (1kg)	2 lb
1.5kg	3 lb

Measures

Metric	Approx Imp Equiv
25ml	1 fl oz
50ml	2 fl oz
125-150ml	1/4 pint (5 fl oz/1 gill)
250-300ml	1/2 pint
375-450ml	3/4 pint
500-600ml	1 pint (20 fl oz)
750-900ml	1 1/2 pints
1-1.25 litres	1 3/4-2 pints
1.4-1.75 litres	3 pints